Hustling and Bustling
HELICOPTERS

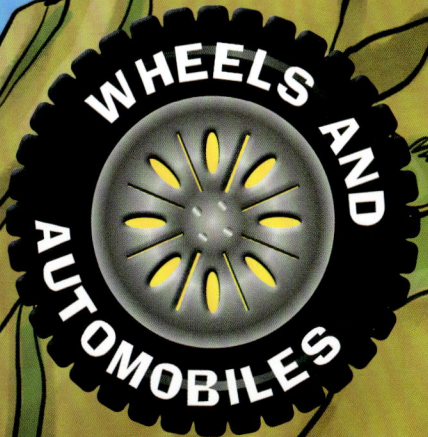

FOX EYE
PUBLISHING

WHEELS AND AUTOMOBILES

Helicopters are helpful machines.
They can do many things.

They help police to patrol the skies and lift heavy loads to the top of buildings.

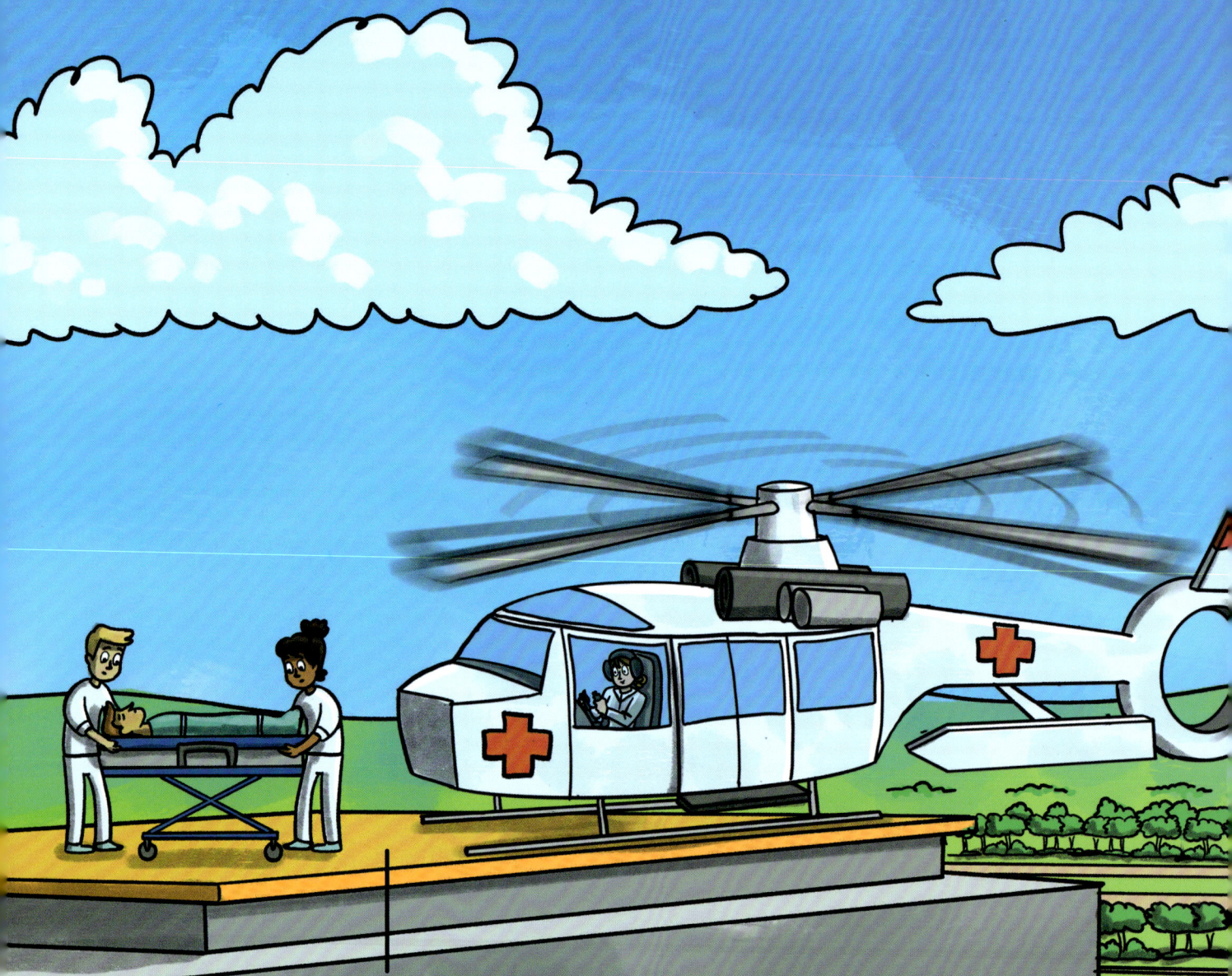

helipad

Helicopters carry patients to the hospital helipad.

They rescue people from the sea and
from mountain slopes on land.

A helicopter is a machine that lifts people into the sky.

Up and up and up it goes until it's flying high.

Helicopters have engines. It gives them power to move.

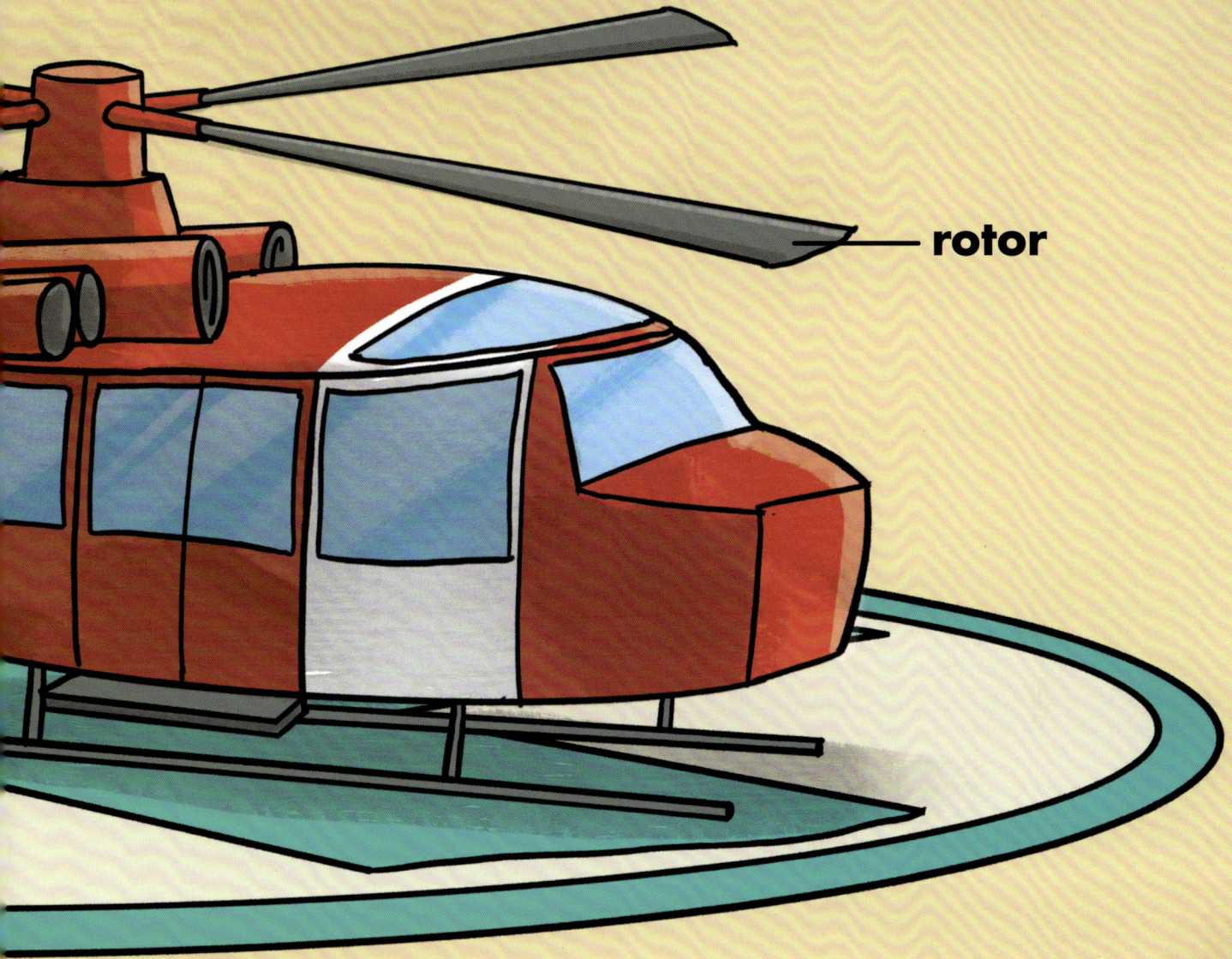

rotor

The engine spins the rotors on the helicopter's roof.

The helicopter's rotors spin so fast, around and around.

As they spin, they lift the helicopter straight up off the ground.

The pilot in the cockpit spins the rotors fast with the controls.

cockpit

pilot

This takes the helicopter higher.
Slowing the rotors takes it low.

The control column and tail rotor
turn the helicopter left or right.

It turns so quickly around the bends,
it really is a sight!

The pilot gets a message on her radio. A sailor is lost in a stormy sea! To the rescue she must go!

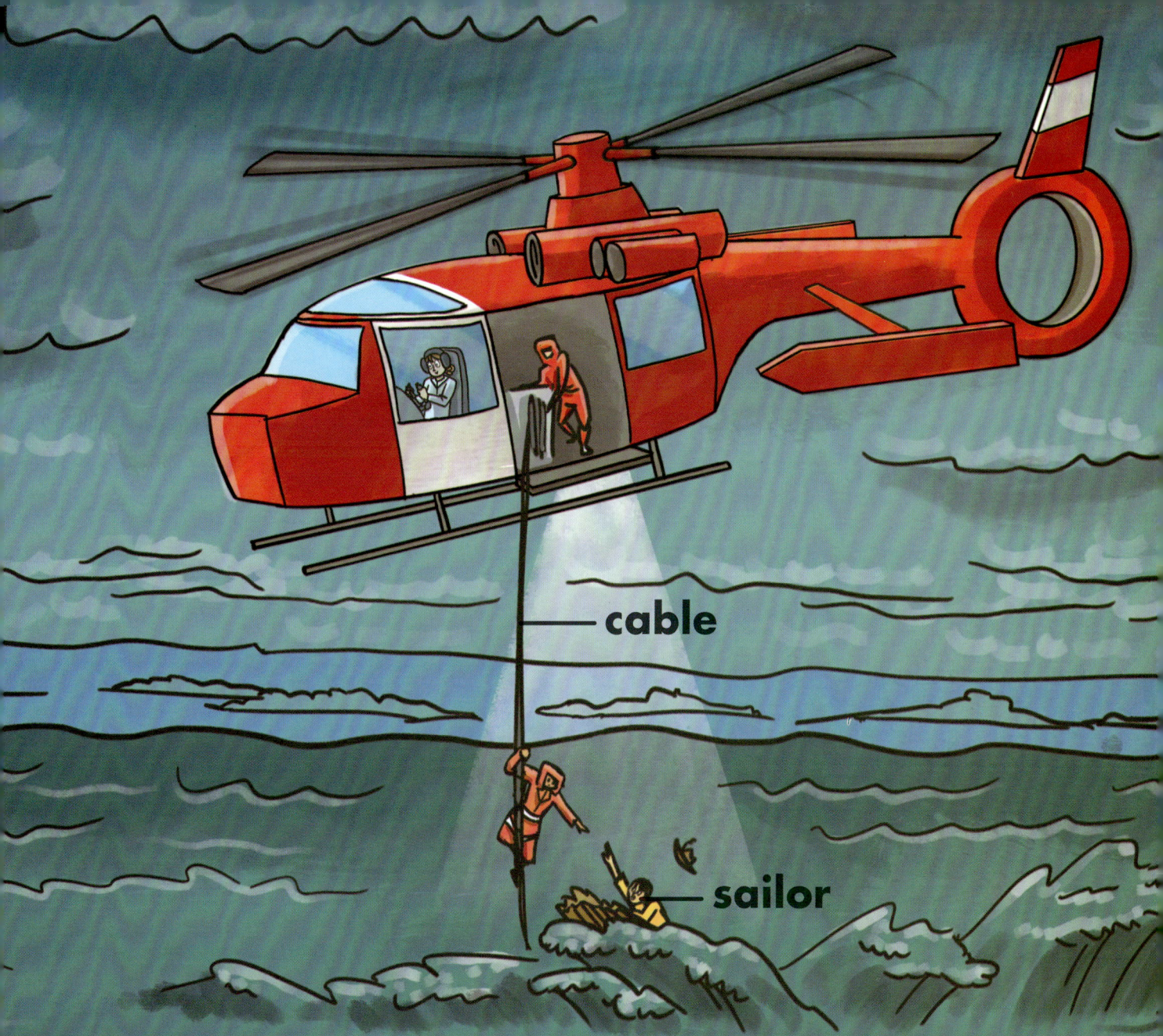

cable

sailor

The pilot spots the sailor. A cable is lowered down.
The helicopter hovers. The waves crash all around.

rescue person

The rescue person is very brave.
He is lowered down to the crashing waves.

The rescuer reaches out and firmly grabs the sailor's hand.
The helicopter lifts them up and carries them back to land.

Inside, the grateful sailor shakes the rescuer by the hand. The helicopter lifts them up and carries them back to land.

The sailor has been rescued from the stormy sea. Thanks to the helpful helicopter and the amazing rescue team!

Bustling Words

A **cable** is a long piece of wire.

A **cockpit** is the part of a helicopter that the pilot sits in.

A **control column** is used by a pilot to steer a helicopter.

Engines are parts of machines where energy is made.

Hovers means staying in one place in the air.

A **machine** helps us to do work.

A **pilot** is a person who flies a helicopter.

Power is energy to do something.

A **radio** is used by a pilot to talk to people outside of a helicopter.

Rescue means to save someone from danger.

Rotors are long, thin blades that spin. As they spin, they lift the helicopter into the air.

Stormy means having bad weather, such as wind and rain.

A **tail rotor** is a group of small blades that spin to move a helicopter left or right.

First published in 2024 by Fox Eye Publishing
Unit 31, Vulcan House Business Centre,
Vulcan Road, Leicester, LE5 3EF
www.foxeyepublishing.com

Author: Katherine Eason
Art director: Paul Phillips
Cover designer: Emma Bailey
Editor: Jenny Rush

All illustrations by Eszter Szepvolgyi

978-1-80445-341-4

Printed in China